"In an age of instant gratification, one-night-stands, and uninspired sex, it is downright refreshing to find a book about sex and integrity for single people."

— Alice S. Umbach, M.S.W.
  Licensed Clinical Social Worker

"Dr. Shaw is not only knowledgeable about human sexuality and how to make it work, she has a kind heart, an honest mind, and twinkling eyes. She has given us a handbook which I know from my own experience is a powerful medium whether used in privacy, with friends, or with professional guidance."

— Leonard Schwartzburd, Ph.D.
  CEO and Director of Psychological Services
  The Clinical Institute of Behavioral Medicine
  Berkeley, California

"The Handbook for Singles brings out particularly important points, such as one does not need a partner to be a sexual person, and celibacy is an acceptable, occasionally preferable, status. I applaud this work!"

— Kitty LaPerriere, Ph.D.
  Past President, American Family Therapy Association

Journey
Toward Intimacy
A Handbook for Singles

Jeanne Shaw, Ph.D.

Couples Enrichment Institute
P. O. Box 420114
Atlanta, Georgia 30342-0114

Journey Toward Intimacy
A Handbook for Singles

Jeanne Shaw, Ph.D.

Published by:

The Couples Enrichment Institute
P.O. Box 420114
Atlanta, Georgia 30342-0114

Printed in the United States of America

ISBN 1-891257-07-2

CONTENTS

Warning — Disclaimer

This book is meant to provide information to individuals on the subject matter covered. It is sold with the understanding that the publisher and author are not engaged in rendering professional services through this handbook. Although the handbook may be used in conjunction with therapy, it does not take the place of therapy. If counseling is required, a *licensed* mental health professional should be contracted.

It is not within the scope of this handbook to provide complete information on the topic. You are urged to read available material about sexual relationships, including celibacy, and tailor the information to your needs. For more material, please see the Appendix, Suggested Readings.

Every effort has been made to make this handbook concise and accurate. However, there may be mistakes, both typographical and in content. Further, standards of sexual behavior change with social change; thus, some concepts basic to this handbook may shift over time.

The purpose of this handbook is to educate and inspire you to fulfill your human potential. The author and publisher shall have neither liability nor responsibility to any individual or couple with respect to any loss or damage caused, or alleged to have been caused, directly or indirectly, by the use of the information contained herein.

If you do not wish to be bound by the above, you may return this book to the publisher, unused, for a full refund.

Welcome to the Handbook!

This handbook is for people who want to explore new ways of being single and sexual, with safety and responsibility. It is also for single people looking for partners and possibilities. Although bookstores are brimming with books promoting ever stronger and longer orgasms through sexual fantasies, sex techniques, sex toys, and masturbation, this one is different. Here, the focus and purpose is your mental, emotional, and physical connection with yourself, not on producing orgasms. This handbook declares that being sexual reflects *who you are*, not what you do.

Sexual terminology can be confusing. The word "sexual" is used in this handbook to mean a feeling of aliveness, an enthusiasm for life, and a way to express that enthusiasm. Being sexual is different from doing sex. You do not need a partner to be sexual or to feel alive, however much you might yearn for one. The term "genital" is used here to mean physical arousal, feeling "horny," a desire for pleasure and release. Genital arousal feels urgent for some, some of the time, especially people under thirty-something. For others, including midlifers and beyond, it means a chance to relish familiar sensations without needing to do anything about them.

Sexual arousal can also be channelled toward creative energy. Of course, serving the urge with a timely, self-administered orgasm is always an option; fortunately, the emotional urge can remain even after the muscle contractions have finished. Sexual energy can be expended without a partner in many ways. This handbook was written with such energy!

If you miss having a sex partner, you are in good company; single people often feel physically and emotionally deprived of sex, more so when they are around couples who seem sexual. Many cultures view single status as incomplete, deficient, or both, particularly during childbearing years. We are taught to shame *ourselves* as deficient if we are single, as though having a partner somehow completes you as a person. Unfortunately, your biological clock concurs even if your intent is to remain childless. When your body gives you maternal or paternal feelings and you know you do not want to make a baby, you are experiencing the instinct that perpetuates the species. It does subside with time, although the portion of the life cycle you are missing still needs to be acknowledged, whether or not you have minimal or deep regret. The important fact is that you are complete as you are simply because you are human.

The goal of this handbook is to acknowledge your wholeness. Your primary relationship is, after all, with yourself. Whether you reject, tolerate, or accept yourself as complete, you will attract friends and potential partners of similar values. Self-respecting, self-reliant, self-accepting people usually find each other. They have a head start creating love relationships precisely because of their ability to love and partner *themselves*.

Solo status can be by choice or by circumstance. Either way, a priority of being single is finding acceptance and pleasure in your relationship with yourself. Accepting yourself solo helps you relish fresh aspects of life, such as your expanding maturity, integrity, and emotional skills. However, feeling whole *alone* can be challenging for the person who desires a partner or who feels incomplete or lonely without someone with whom to share life. Bonding is human and natural. Yearning to have a partner is human and natural, too.

It is human nature to pair off; yet, some people do not know how to, not everybody wants to, and circumstances are not always available, in which case partnering yourself may be your only option. Still, you do not have to relinquish your sexuality any more than you have to give up your curiosity, creativity, or playfulness. Your sexuality reflects who you are. Your sexual behavior is what you do. There is a difference between who you are and what you do: *Who you are is not negotiable.*

Thirty years of observing and working with sexually satisfied and unsatisfied solo and partnered adults has provided a wealth of practical guidelines. These guidelines are presented here in the form of exercises for you to do alone, with friends, or benevolent others.

These exercises have been designed to explore sexuality from perspectives that are unusual in American culture. People report that working through the exercises alone or with friends is rewarding, promising, and awkward even without genital or physical focus. Although there is no wrong way to approach the exercises, following the suggested guidelines in sequence will enrich your journey.

Guidelines

1. Read the suggestions at the beginning of each exercise.

2. Make enough time to read and reflect. Set aside responses for a while--a few hours or days--and return later with an inquiring mind.

3. Don't explode, don't cave in, and don't give up. Just quiet yourself. This means to contain and monitor your responses and reactions, not stifle them.

4. After each exercise, think about how it was for you to reflect on the topic at hand. This is practice in self-awareness.

Good Journey!

Purposes

1. Observe how your beliefs, attitudes, and personality affect your sexuality.

2. Learn how accepting yourself without a sexual partner can be part of living your life with enthusiasm.

3. Recognize the thoughts, feelings, and behaviors that enhance or block sexual energy and self-expression.

4. Explore the significance of anxiety-reducing behaviors (safe, familiar, comfortable) and anxiety-inducing behaviors (adventurous, unfamiliar, uncomfortable).

5. Explore your inherent ability to partner yourself.

6. Use ambivalence and contradiction for personal growth.

7. Learn how validation from another person comforts you and how self-validation builds confidence and maturity.

8. Explore maturity, integrity, self-respect, and intimacy.

My wish in completing this handbook:

My wish for my future:

I am open to new ideas about my sexuality:

☐ Yes, and:

☐ Not really, I'm:

☐ No way, but I'll read on just in case . . .

Sexual Attitudes

The first exercise is a survey of your sexual attitudes. A survey helps you become more aware of what you think, feel, and value. Please don't judge your responses but use them to increase self-awareness and sexual choices. Knowing your sexual attitudes gives you choices about how you want to express your thoughts, feelings, and behavior. Being unaware leaves you at the mercy of attitudes that can serve you poorly. Whether you express your sexuality through celibacy, creativity, masturbation, longing, or partner-sex, awareness increases your options.

Observing your sexual attitudes and beliefs will let you know what serves you and what defeats you, what energizes you and what drains you. Childhood guidelines and rules about being male or female form the basis of your present thoughts, feelings, and behaviors about sex. Restructuring self-defeating beliefs in favor of expanding your thinking is a real option *now*. Many people feel nervous about exploring their sexual attitudes because, as children, we learned to frame sexuality in moral, negative, and value-laden terms. Sometimes, other people's values caused shame about our bodies, natural feelings, and developing urges. Learning how to contain your urges and choose your behavior is an opportunity to relinquish shame and take charge of yourself.

Shame, fear, and negative attitudes about body parts and sex causes anxiety, spaciness, and disconnection from yourself. Disconnection inhibits your liveliness, while spaciness blocks your presence. Presence is required for sexual energy and for feeling solid inside yourself. It is important to be present for yourself, conscious about your anxiety. Even though you may not understand why you feel a certain way, accepting that your feelings exist enlivens you and helps you engage people. A good place to start is attitudes, values, and beliefs about sex.

Suggestions:

1. Complete the Sexual Attitude Survey quickly and spontaneously.

2. When you finish, ask yourself: What feelings and thoughts are stirred? Are they familiar? What might your particular attitudes reveal about your past? Present? Future?

3. You learn most when you feel uncomfortable about a topic. Discomfort stimulates opportunity for self-awareness. Comfort is also necessary, but it does not stimulate change. Notice which statements in this exercise are neutral, comfortable and uncomfortable.

4. Don't explode, don't cave in, and don't give up. Just quiet yourself. Change is not imperative. Simply becoming aware of possibilities may be enough to give you more options.

5. Select a few sexual attitudes you responded to with approval or disapproval. Note whether you could or would discuss them with a friend or potential partner. Discussing responses with friends gives you information about your uniqueness and your similarity.

Sexual Attitude Survey

Please indicate whether you agree (A) or disagree (D).

(   ) 1. Sex is perfect, there is nothing I need to change.

(   ) 2. At this stage in my life I am familiar with my body, how it functions, and how technically skilled I am.

(   ) 3. Sexual pleasure is natural and should come easily.

(   ) 4. I enjoy feeling sexually aroused with and without a partner.

(   ) 5. I often wonder if I will find a committed partner with mutual caring, interests, and goals.

(   ) 6. I feel very alone and lonely without a partner.

(   ) 7. I want a partner for sex, not for a relationship.

(   ) 8. At times in my life I have behaved sexually when I really did not want to, just to please someone.

(   ) 9. I really get into being aroused by my sexual fantasy.

(   ) 10. I enjoy making love to myself whenever I like.

(   ) 11. Life is too short to be embarrassed about sex.

(   ) 12. I can enjoy many sexual activities with a partner, especially when we forego penetration.

(   ) 13. I enjoy feeling sexual with another person even though I do not (often, ever) act on those feelings.

(   ) 14. I know how to plan ahead for a safe experience which does not include exchange of body fluids.

(   ) 15. I would not consider "exchanging fluids" or having penetrating sex outside of a committed relationship.

(   ) 16. I am celibate and appreciate my strong values.

(   ) 17. I miss sex because I have not been able to find a suitable partner.

(   ) 18. I have never really enjoyed partner sex.

(   ) 19. I have never really felt closely connected to the person I had (or wanted) sex with.

(   ) 20. I want sex no matter how or who.

(   ) 21. I hate this survey.

(   ) 22. I want to consider this question:

Common Misinformed Beliefs About Sex

The next few pages list common misbeliefs about sex. You may think some are true, depending on how, when, and where you grew up. However, they are all erroneous beliefs, any one of which can impede your sexual growth. This exercise explores whether a change of attitude might be advantageous.

Almost everyone in our culture learns to think in ways that undermine natural sexuality. But people can restructure their attitudes with accurate information and open minds. You may benefit from reading a good sex education book. Your clergy, public and university libraries, SIECUS, AASECT (see Appendix), and almost any bookstore can locate a reliable sex education reference. Sexual education is neither pornography nor erotica, it is just a way to learn about sexual behavior, adult choice, and personal responsibility.

Suggestions:

1. According to your present belief, mark each statement in the first list as true or false. The commentary that follows will bring you up to date.

2. Notice whether you disagree with the statements and how your objections affect your thinking. Are you uncomfortable thinking you might be wrong about a fact? Do you appreciate being brought up to date?

3. Don't explode, don't cave in, and don't give up. Just quiet yourself.

4. Note how you feel when you consider your sexual misconceptions. Are you open to different perspectives?

Common Misinformed Beliefs about Sex

☐ When she's wet, she's ready.

☐ Unless he has an erection, he doesn't care.

☐ Foreplay is for women, intercourse is for men.

☐ If you love and communicate well, sex will be good.

☐ A sexual problem means something is wrong with you.

☐ Casual sex is more exciting than intimate sex.

☐ In a good relationship you have a fulfilling sexual experience every time.

☐ After age 25 your sex drive begins to decrease and stops altogether by 65.

☐ Initiating sex is a masculine privilege.

☐ If either partner is aroused, sex must follow.

☐ Having "G" spot and multiple orgasms means a woman has "been around."

☐ Menopause decreases sexual desire.

☐ When you lose desire for the partner you have, it is time to look for a different partner.

☐ A man with a large penis is sexually skilled.

☐ Women with large breasts are easily aroused.

☐ People in committed relationships do not masturbate.

☐ Once you know the sexual ropes you are set for life.

☐ The best sex is spontaneous and unplanned.

☐ Penis-in-vagina is the only sex that really counts.

☐ Great sex happens when you close your eyes, have a fantasy, and produce an orgasm.

☐ If I can't make him/her come, I'm not performing well.

☐ Celibate people eventually lose the ability to have sex with a partner.

Notes

Commentary on Misinformed Beliefs

When she's wet she's ready. Some women get wet when they get aroused, but not all do. Some get wet before they have an awareness of arousal, and others feel intensely aroused without lubricating. Most of us learned this inaccuracy in high school.

Unless he has an erection he doesn't care. Getting an erection means only that his erectile tissue is working. He can get an erection and still not care. He can even get an erection and not be sexually aroused. Many conditions can inhibit erections, e.g., medications, performance anxiety, fear, depression, bereavement, medical problems. And yes, his penis may, in fact, be saying what he is not revealing in words, that he doesn't like you anymore.

Foreplay is for women, intercourse for men. Foreplay communicates what will happen next and how it will happen. To portray women as dependent romantics and men as aggressive or avoidant of arousal is a disservice to both. Many, if not most, men love foreplay (*boys* like the relief of a quick orgasm), and many women enjoy humping with a penis inside.

If you love and communicate well, sex will be good. Not for over half of America's loving, communicating couples with sexual dissatisfactions. Communication is necessary but not sufficient for creating erotic sex. Emotional maturity, self-respect, integrity, and willingness are necessary.

A sexual problem means something is wrong with you. If the problem has no physical cause, it is a signal that you are ripe for change and growth. A problem can be the result of erroneous learning, self-defeating attitudes, anxiety, depression, shame, abuse, malnutrition, fatigue, alcohol, drug and tobacco overuse, stress, disinterest, etc., all reasons for examining your personal beliefs, values, and wishes.

Casual sex is more exciting than intimate sex. Almost nothing is more exciting or induces more anxiety than erotic sex between long-term partners. Casual sex can be stunningly exciting until it gets boring in its sameness. Behavior can get monotonous, but growing in the experience of yourself keeps you juicy.

In a good sexual relationship you have a fulfilling experience every time. Like everything else in life, sex has cycles of ebb and flow, contact and withdrawal. Sexual experience depends on individuals, their maturity, integrity, age, health, emotions, fatigue, stress, life circumstances, and more. Sex can be disappointing, monotonous, adequate, delightful, stunning, and ecstatic. Sex depends on so many variables, the wonder is that it ever happens well.

After age 25 your sex drive begins to decrease and stops altogether by 65. Sex drive depends more on maturity, integrity, and an available partner, than age. Older women, whose skill and personal confidence often increase with age, may have more sex drive than ever, post-menopause. Aging men have biological changes, but sexual pleasure remains. Men often grow more sensual as they age. Sexual energy stops altogether with death, not at any particular age.

Initiating sex is a masculine duty. Actually, it is human to initiate sex. Everyone has both masculine and feminine qualities. It is now politically correct for either partner to initiate, and also not to initiate.

If either partner is aroused, intercourse must follow. The unfounded belief that people cannot or should not control sexual urges is a myth brought forth from the pre-WWII era to protect men and women from their sexual feelings. Men and women have the capability to enjoy the urge and do nothing about it or masturbate to orgasm if they want brief pleasure and release. However, it is not necessary to top arousal off with intercourse or orgasm.

Having "G" spot and multiple orgasms means a woman has "been around." Women often want to learn how their G-spot works when they discover it's existence (see the Suggested Readings section in the appendix). "Been around" is a judgment, not an observation; G-spot and multiple orgasms is a learned skill for women. Many teach it to themselves.

Menopause decreases sexual desire and arousal. Decreasing estrogen levels can raise, lower, or have no effect on desire and arousal. This is one of the feminine mysteries.

When you lose desire for the partner you have, it is time to look for another partner. Loss of desire signals your opportunity to mature in this relationship, whether that means leave or stay. When you leave a relationship, it should be from a sense of completion, not because you are not being fed sexually. Sexual desire is less a measure of connectedness with a partner than it is with yourself.

A man with a big penis is sexually skilled. The size of a penis does not predict level of sexual energy or skill except in fantasy and pornographic media.

Women with large breasts are easily aroused. Breast size does not predict arousability. Some nipples are arousable, some not, and some are some of the time. Size (amount of fatty tissue) is not a physical factor, although the cultural value of large breasts may incline women to feel sexually desirable.

People in committed relationships do not masturbate. Of course they do, or most do, but they may not bring it up for discussion. Masturbation is not a substitute for partner sex, it is legitimate sex-for-one. Include your partner anytime, and continue to enjoy making love to yourself.

23

Once you know the sexual ropes you are set for life. Adolescent boys like to believe this. You are set only in that you acknowledge you must learn each partner, over time, repeatedly. This makes you a good learner and growing lover.

The best sex is spontaneous and unplanned. People without children, pets, or jobs believe this. Even spontaneous sex is planned, e.g., you brush your teeth or wear sexy underwear. The best sex is planned by both partners, with anticipation. And yes, great sex happens unexpectedly, too.

Penis-in-vagina is the only sex that really counts. This is a sexist (and heterosexist) goal-oriented opinion that gives men the anxiety that he is only as valuable as his erect penis, and she as her receptive, wet vagina.

Great sex happens when you close your eyes, have a fantasy, and produce an orgasm. You are not connected with your partner when you focus on a fantasy. This is masturbatory sex and one-night-stand behavior.

If I cannot make him or her come, I am not performing well. Although your partner's orgasm is not your responsibility, you are responsible for your technical, social, and emotional skill. Your genitals are body parts to use for pleasure and expression of love, not reassurance.

Celibate people eventually lose the ability to have sex alone and with a partner. Celibate people have the capacity to use sexual energy so that it doesn't make them feel "horny." The "use it or lose it" notion is only accurate temporarily, for people of all ages. Masturbation techniques and falling in love again help resolve problems of disuse, when and if it happens.

Wake-up Calls

Every individual has effective and ineffective ways to prepare for change. Unfortunately, we don't always realize how our behavior is ineffective or puts people off. For example, you may express irritation (passivity, fear, neediness, intimidation, rigidity, etc.), someone remarks about it, and you respond with surprise, annoyance, or anxiety. Thinking about the way you behave and seeing yourself as you come across to others can help you make contact without alienating people.

There is no magic formula for becoming aware of your behavior and how you affect people. When you are willing to gain insight or get feedback, you learn. When you ignore your own self-defeating behavior, your friends and family may not have the courage or skills to tell you how you affect them, or maybe you ignore their complaints when they tell you. Their offer of constructive feedback can be an uncomfortable gift that you can use to learn, change, and be happier with yourself.

What, exactly, is a wake-up call? It is a subtle or obvious tension inside yourself, and/or feedback from others, that alerts you to objectionable behavior that, when changed, allows you to get more of what you want in relationships. How you express yourself and behave toward others can affect you and your relationships adversely or productively. How you respond to situations and people reflects your level of perception and self-respect. Your ability to be a competent adult in charge of your own continuing development is reflected in the way you relate to yourself and respond to others.

There are many kinds of wake-up calls. If you see yours on the following lists, use the information to observe how you help people avoid contact with you. Wake-up calls happen to everybody; what you do with them shows you how you grow or stagnate. Awakening to your own behavior can increase your options for sexual enrichment as well as partnering.

Suggestions:

1. Read the list and check each characteristic you believe fits or nearly fits you. Read the list as though you were someone else who knows you well, or ask someone to check the list honestly with you.

2. Think about your responses. Notice whether you open yourself to insight, contain yourself, or respond with counter-arguments.

3. Don't explode, don't cave in, and don't give up. Just quiet yourself. This is a difficult, self-revealing exercise.

4. Afterwards, think about what it was like to consider your own wake-up calls. Could you discuss this exercise with a close friend? A group? A partner?

Wake-up Calls

- [ ] I am rarely around affectionate people.

- [ ] I have sex and regret it later.

- [ ] I spend dissatisfying hours alone, not by choice.

- [ ] I spend time with people and I still feel alone.

- [ ] I feel shy, afraid, or inhibited about social contact.

- [ ] I sometimes get argumentative, critical, or distant.

- [ ] I try to make contact but people shy away from me.

- [ ] I often blame or shame myself or others.

- [ ] I can usually find the negative aspect of anything.

- [ ] I withdraw when I get scared, nervous, or irritated.

- [ ] Contact depends on other people's behavior, not mine.

- [ ] I often feel contemptuous or sarcastic toward others.

- [ ] People are occasionally offended by my bluntness.

- [ ] If I can get away with something, I will.

- [ ] I am emotionally dishonest and manipulative.

- [ ] I have been known to place a big guilt-trip on people.

- [ ] I cannot tolerate rejection under any circumstances.

- [ ] I often say I agree when I don't, to keep the peace.

- [ ] I overwork, overeat, overspend, gamble money I don't have, or overuse drugs.

- [ ] I have affairs with other people's partners.

- [ ] I am a horny person and will not stifle my genital behavior no matter what the circumstances.

Waking Up

- [ ] I can disagree gently.

- [ ] I can negotiate for behavior change (mine) with good will.

- [ ] I recognize the fact that nobody is innocent.

- [ ] I stay focused on, and discuss, my own experience.

- [ ] I am not manipulated to do what serves me poorly.

- [ ] I think twice before I act as though I have no control.

- [ ] I act toward others with kindness and compassion.

- [ ] I do this even when nobody else co-operates.

- [ ] I choose integrity, self-respect, and good will, mostly.

- [ ] I tolerate my own growth even when I'm anxious.

- [ ] I expect to lose friends when I hurt them repeatedly.

- [ ] I expect to lose friends when I stop being their crutch.

- [ ] I realize that I am the person with whom I will spend the rest of my life.

Finding and Being the Right Partner

List four personality traits important to you in a partner:

1.

2.

3.

4.

List four behaviors important to you in a partner:

1.

2.

3.

4.

List four values a person must have to attract you:

1.

2.

3.

4.

List four of your own personality traits:

1.

2.

3.

4.

List four of your own relationship-building behaviors:

1.

2.

3.

4.

List four of your own values that attract people:

1.

2.

3.

4.

Compare who you are with whom you want for a partner. You will almost invariably attract—and be attracted to—someone who is a perfect fit for who you are now. A "perfect fit" means you can push each other's growth with great energy after the romanic stage wears off. The relevant question is: "How do I develop *myself* to be the person I want to be, in this relationship?" No matter how hard you try or how noble your intentions, you cannot change the other person, so you might as well focus on the only person you can change: yourself.

If you attract and are attracted to the "wrong" kind of person, you are looking into your dark side emotional mirror. Take a good look at yourself in relationship to "wrong" partners. For example, who but a "masochist" is attracted to a "sadist?" Who but a "victim" can repeatedly find "persecutors?" Who but a "needy parent" will find a "Peter-Pan" to take care of?

If you want to attract a person with the qualities you listed (there is no way around this) you must know which qualities in yourself you want (and don't want) in another. People in emotional pain really do find each other, e.g., depressives often attract people with high energy, "I'll-save-you," impossible ideals. Alcoholics often attract lenient, emotionally needy people who initially seem strong and giving. The partner of a person with problems in living can seem well-adjusted by comparison. Successful people, like mature people, often attract each other. Yes, emotional and behavioral opposites do attract, just as similars attract. Nonetheless, the partner you like best will be very close to your level of emotional development.

You will have daily, or maybe hourly, opportunities to struggle with your integrity in any sexual relationship. This is natural. No matter who your partner is, you will have a chance to grow yourself up more than you ever thought you could or would. Fortunately, struggling and achieving integrity, wholeness, completeness, competence, and self-respect in relationship makes sexual energy bountiful. And, if you do not find the "right" partner, at the very least you become the right partner. Just as your sexual self appreciates your life energy, your deeper self appreciates the connection you make with your soul.

Notes

Characteristics of Sexual Aliveness

Many qualities make for sexual aliveness. Genetic, biological, circadian, religious, personality, character, personal and family history, and individual differences make each one of us unique. Even so, common qualities are required to sustain sexual energy. One of the most important is emotional maturity, the characteristic with which we take charge of ourselves as adults. Emotional maturity includes the capability to:

- Define yourself to others because you know who you are.

- Admit you're wrong or off-base when you are.

- Soothe your own anxiety, insecurity, helplessness, rage.

- Validate your own feelings.

- Manage conflict without avoiding it.

- Observe and regulate your own behavior.

- Stay connected to friends for many years.

- Verify yourself as whole and separate from others.

- Value togetherness as much as separateness.

- Do these without exploding, caving in, or giving up.

Mature people can speak their truth with compassion, manage their own anxiety, choose their behavior, and divulge their joy, hurt, anger, fear, and other feelings with friends and prospective partners in appropriate ways and circumstances. Making room for themselves in a relationship, they can accept the results of their disclosures. Good will and self-respect are the foundations of mental, emotional, and physical relating.

In the next exercise, you will clarify your own requirements for being or becoming more sexually alive. Consider how much and which qualities are your own and which you would like to enhance. Add whatever qualities are missing. Note that, although "romance" is important, it is not included here because it is a term often confused with dependency and child-like attachment based on need instead of fullness and maturity.

Having a partner is not a requirement for feeling sexually alive. Recent surveys indicate that many midlife single, divorced, and widowed people actively maintain and enjoy their freedom, independence, and sexuality, with and without partners. Many well-adjusted younger men and women do not choose to be in an ongoing, committed relationship. Although they may be open to one, they are not searching actively because solo life is satisfying and fulfilling.

Suggestions:

1. Consider each quality on the list and how this is and is not similar to your own.

2. If your life feels dull or diminished, focus on your own dullness and how your choices drain or diminish you.

3. Don't explode, don't cave in, and don't give up. Just quiet yourself.

4. Think about what it was like to consider the qualities that enliven or deepen your relationship to yourself.

Characteristics of Sexual Aliveness

- Sense of humor.

- Joy, play, and laughter.

- Self-respect (ability to love and be loved).

- Affectionate, sensual, and sexual energy.

- Presence.

- Closeness (predictability, comfort, familiarity).

- Intimacy (unpredictability, emotional risk-taking, newness).

- Valuing emotional separateness.

- Valuing emotional togetherness.

- Maturity (self-responsible, self-validating, self-soothing).

- Completeness and wholeness.

Notes

Productive Disclosure

One of the most difficult conversations is the one where people tell, or don't tell, what's really going on, sexually and otherwise. Telling *yourself* what is going on is a basic necessity but hard to do when you don't believe you know. This is one reason why self-awareness is so important and so difficult.

"I don't want to hurt his feelings or push him away." "I'm afraid she might get angry or leave." People protect each other by not speaking their truth. People, similarly, protect themselves by hiding their own truth without even being aware that they are hiding from themselves, or that these unknowns can affect their ability to connect. "Pretend the issue isn't here and it will go away" is becoming a politically correct philosophy in the U.S.

Talking about who you are enhances your chance to get to know yourself and each other. Initiating a self-revealing conversation is hard enough when you're talking to yourself and downright intense when you're speaking with another person. Although discretion toward yourself is neither useful nor necessary, it is wise to speak with discretion to a new friend or potential lover. Saying the easy things first and the hard things later go a long way toward making and keeping new friends. As you begin to speak your truth in small increments, the person you want to know better can respond without feeling put off by heavy initial disclosures. Wait to tell your secrets until you know each other. But tell your secrets to yourself anytime.

Many things can undermine initial contacts and established friendships. Two, for example, are need for approval and fear of rejection. Almost everybody *wants* approval and acceptance; the key is being able to give them to yourself when you think you *need* them. Self-support helps you risk and manage rejection and disappointment from others. Managing rejection from others is valuable experience and gives you better judgment for the future. You can learn to hear "no" and handle feeling rejected, devastated, and getting your ego bruised.

Friendship takes time. Willingness to be present fully will help you get started. You can give or get a gift of disclosure whether or not you elect to use the information in the service of building a friendship or sexual relationship.

Although sexual energy advances in a relationship with verbal and emotional contact, body parts do not have to touch physically to be enjoyable. Celibacy is a self-respecting (and sexual tension-building) choice. It is the only choice for some. It is also embraced by proponents who declare that temporary celibacy keeps the sexual energy strong long after a marriage takes place. On the other hand, celibate people who expect marriage or other commitments to resolve sexual knowledge, skill, and attitude problems will surely be disappointed.

Self-respect is behaving in good faith with yourself without guessing how others might prefer that you behave. Integrity, (emotional wholeness) is built on self-respect, and lasting sexual energy in relationship is built on integrity. Therefore, your level of sexual energy can indicate how connected you are with yourself, how whole you feel as an individual.

Suggestions:

1. Fill out the Disclosure Checklist by yourself. As you read your responses, note whether you could or would make these disclosures to a nonsexual friend or sexual partner.

2. Don't explode, don't cave in, and don't give up. Just quiet yourself.

3. Think for a few minutes about what it is like for you to consider this topic, and what you might learn about yourself if you explored further.

Disclosure Checklist

1. When I feel anxious about behaving sexually, I . . .

2. Being touched affectionately feels . . .

3. Being touched sexually feels . . .

4. When I feel or behave sexually with someone I know, I . . .

5. When I feel sexual or behave genitally with a stranger or a near-stranger, I . . .

6. I feel something special during sex when I . . .

7. I feel "careful" with a partner when . . .

8. My body is . . .

9. If I enjoyed (liked, respected) me more, I might . . .

10. I would turn on more intensely if I . . .

11. For me, sex is . . .

12. I can tell when a person's body is with me and their spirit is somewhere else, by . . .

13. At times I would like to get primitive and lustful . . .

14. I'm afraid a new partner will/won't tell me when they dislike something, and then . . .

15. If I ask someone to change what they're doing . . .

16. I have a hard time finding a match for my candor and my uninhibited enjoyment of sex . . .

17. Sex is/isn't fun for me, so I . . .

18. I sometimes pretend orgasm so that I . . .

19. When I get the nerve I will . . .

20. Being the type of person I am, I probably will not . . .

21. For me, masturbation is . . .

22. I sometimes have sex because, if I don't, . . .

23. I have had an AIDS test and always ask a prospective partner if he or she has, and what the results were, as . . .

24. My checklist needs to include:

Sexual Scripts

Each of us learns as a child how to behave in order to be accepted by families, peers, and society. We receive important positive and negative spoken and unspoken messages about how to think, feel, and behave according to the current social rules. Parents, teachers, and other adults determine the boundaries of our young minds; their unspoken directives tell us unmistakably which topics and behaviors are off-limits.

This is how children receive "sexual scripts," subconscious directions for how to behave and feel about sex. We then grow up feeling and behaving in a prescribed manner, without a clue that our scripts direct our sexual feelings and behavior. An example of one kind of script is that sex is in the realm of sacred pleasure and should only be developed physically in a committed relationship. Another kind of script is the notion that sex is dirty and disgusting, but save it for someone you love (!?), or do it in the dark because sex is dirty and shameful. A common script about body image urges us to judge a beautifully functioning body as imperfect when it doesn't meet current "thinness" criteria for women or "penis length" criteria for men. Everyone carries unknown scripts that affect thoughts, feelings, and behavior.

Parents, for whatever reasons, often tell children about reproduction but rarely about sexual intimacy. Consequently, many children grow up believing sex is a taboo topic when, in fact, it is simply a topic their parents were uncomfortable discussing. The ancient taboo prevents timely, knowledgeable, and appropriate conversations about sexuality, arousal, orgasm, desire, masturbation, childhood sexual abuse, sexually transmitted diseases, shame, and on the other hand, self-satisfaction in conducting oneself according to family values. Believing sex is a taboo topic is not only an obstacle in a committed relationship, it can be life-threatening or harmful for partners of people who are HIV+ or who have other undisclosed sexually transmitted diseases.

You can uncover your scripts and use the information for personal and relational fulfillment. Scripts, by definition, are hidden from consciousness. Nonetheless, a search for clues can uncover script patterns. Just notice your repetitive behaviors, thoughts, and feelings that result in the same unwanted consequences that, once again, don't let you get what you want. Self-observation, awareness, and insight give you an option to restructure your script and your behavior to fit who you are now. The results can expand your self-respect.

The next exercise helps you observe yourself. If you come upon a blind spot, ask for help, guess, or make up a response. If you do not know what ideas and values you received from parental figures, think about your present values and how you might have learned them.

Suggestions:

1. Write your responses to the Sexual Script items.

2. Bridge your responses to a feeling or pattern you recognize, such as from earlier in your life.

3. Don't explode, don't cave in, and don't give up. Just quiet yourself.

4. What was it like for you to consider your sexual script?

Sexual Script

1. Write a positive idea you received from your mothering figure about sexuality:

2. Write a positive idea you received from your fathering figure about sexuality:

3. Write a negative idea you received from your mothering figure about sexuality:

4. Write a negative idea you received from your fathering figure about sexuality:

5. How do these messages affect your sexual feelings and behavior now, both positively and negatively?

6. If you could change anything about your present sexual (or nonsexual) experience, how do you imagine yourself being different? Which part of this is possible?

7. What would you like your children (or others) to learn about their own sexuality?

Perspectives on Sex

Each generation has its own perspective about sexual behavior, knowledge, attitudes, skill, and experience. Religions have guidelines, communities have customs, families have rules, and peers have accurate and imaginary information. With conflicting guidelines about sex, it is no wonder we grow up confused. In the next exercise, you have an opportunity to clarify further perspectives on your beliefs and attitudes.

Perspectives on sex are offered in two categories: conventional, meaning usual and customary; and unconventional, meaning unusual in today's transitioning, romanticized culture. There is nothing inherently wrong with romance unless we associate it with having a partner to fulfill dependency and security needs. Getting a partner based on neediness is the way many people connect. When you connect with neediness instead of wholeness, expectations of sexual fulfillment haven't a chance. We cannot be sexually fulfilled over time with a partner on whom we overdepend emotionally; this eventually feels incestuous.

Sex in the usual view is seen as natural, not learned. The biological urge to procreate overlaps with the idea that sexual skills and techniques are acquired. Conventional notions cite sex as an appetite that, like hunger, should be fed regularly (by somebody else). This notion overlooks the fact that you can feed yourself and you can be with your partner because you want to, not because you or he/she is needy.

Unconventional perspectives are founded on the idea that maturity and integrity are basic to good sex, and that good sex happens with feelings of fullness, not neediness. In our culture, *mature* love is unconventional! With maturity, partners soothe and feed themselves instead of demanding comfort and service from each other. Paradoxically, self-sufficiency and emotional separateness help partners be of greater comfort and service, help partners bond more, not less, intimately.

Suggestions:

1. Read this exercise carefully. Indicate on each page the perspectives that fit for you.

2. Consider the meaning of each viewpoint, personally and relationally.

3. If you share with a friend or discussion group, note how similar or different your thoughts are from theirs and how different your thinking is or is not after you consider the conventional and unconventional perspectives.

4. Don't explode, don't cave in, and don't give up. Just quiet yourself.

5. Take a few more minutes to consider or discuss what exploring sexual perspectives was like for you.

Perspectives on Sex

Conventional	Unconventional
Sex is a natural hunger.	Good sex is learned, reproductive sex is natural.
The focus is on genitals, techniques, and mechanics.	Focus is on intimate connection and erotic arousal.
Good sex means you focus on a good fantasy and intense physical sensations.	Focus is on your sensations and your partner, not on a disengaging fantasy.
Desire means need and eagerness for orgasm(s).	Desire means eagerness for a partner before, during, and after sex.
For good sex, reduce anxiety and stay relaxed.	For good sex, create high tension and arousal. Relax later.
Orgasms at low levels of arousal are acceptable.	Orgasms occur with intense arousal.
Avoid problems and conflict, "keep the peace."	Problems and conflicts are opportunities for growth.
Get your partner to validate, assure, and protect you.	Validate, motivate, reassure, protect *yourself*.
Security depends on your partner's behavior and opinion.	Security depends on self-soothing, self-validation, and self-respect.
Emotional security is necessary for good sex.	Emotional security depends on self-responsibility.
The main complaint is, "My partner is not giving me what I need in this relationship."	The main complaint is, "I'm not giving myself what I want in this relationship."

Notes

Conversations about Sex

Have you ever had a love relationship when you talked for hours about everything under the sun, believing you would always feel such love, flexibility, and openness? That is the romantic stage, a brief time when the magic of love erases obstacles between lovers. When romantic love feels permanent and stimulating, personal growth feels effortless.

When you grow to know yourself and your partner better in relationship, you will almost certainly encounter disappointment and disillusionment. To see reality instead of illusions—what you want reality to be—is a good thing even though it can be very disappointing. The problem gets bigger when we believe our illusions more than we believe what is.

Love swells and recedes with cycles like everything else in life, and romance defers to real loving as hormones make way for growth. Personal growth is second in complexity only to staying in relationship while you mature. According to divorce statistics, staying connected to a partner as you develop yourself is beyond the ken of more than half of all American couples. The others are trying to figure out how to build a successful relationship by taking on the task of being the partners they want to be in the relationship they have created. And others don't pair off at all, but this doesn't mean their growth stops. They just grow in relationship to themselves.

People with excellent communication skills do not always speak meaningfully about sex. Even alone, we don't often think meaningfully about sex, that is, to discover what sex means personally and relationally. The next exercise may help you experience a meaningful conversation. It can be with yourself, an imaginary partner, someone you dream of just for fun, or a real prospective partner. Even without prospects for a partner, learning more about your expectations of yourself will increase your choices of behaving unexpectedly.

Suggestions:

1. Write your responses and put them away to read later. Remember that the terms "sexual" and "genital" have different meanings.

2. Notice if this exercise is easy, hard, fun, boring, sad, scary, irritating, etc. How do you handle your responses?

3. Don't explode, don't cave in, and don't give up. Just quiet yourself.

Conversations about Sex

1. What I appreciate me for sexually is:

2. One of my most attractive qualities is:

3. I chuckle whenever I think about:

4. A deeply tender moment for me was:

5. One of the toughest times for me genitally was/is:

6. What I learned from that about myself is:

7. If I had a year left to live, I would:

8. When I first became/become genitally active I hoped:

9. I am willing to have sexually revealing conversations when:

10. My hope for the future is:

Dysfunctional Sex, Functional Sex, and Erotic Sex

The usual view of sexual behavior has just two classifications: dysfunctional and functional. This view assumes your choice is genital sex, not celibacy. In any case, these categories refer to your plumbing, not to your experience. Using only "functional" or "dysfunctional" behavior to evaluate sexual being ignores intimate sex and erotic experience with a life-partner.

Intimate, erotic sex is different from lust with an unfamiliar partner. Being unfamiliar is a lusty turn-on for many singles. Erotic intimacy happens when you can tolerate getting what you want with a committed partner. If you want more than functional, adequate, or boring sex in a relationship, you must become adult enough to manage the anxiety that comes with intimacy and erotic behavior. A huge porn industry attests to attempts to juice up boring genital arousal with erotic videos, fantasies, and sex toys, which help until they become boring.

What kind of sex in relationship is not eventually monotonous? The kind that supplies you with joy and fear, desire and anxiety, appreciation and dread, all at the same time. This kind of sex is the result of a willingness to tolerate, for example, your own judgment of your appearance, fear of rejection, anxiety about performance, shame, loss, and impermanence. Restructuring your internal emotional environment by increasing your ability to tolerate these anxieties is a good way to increase your capacity for erotic sex in relationship.

Sex with and without a life partner need not become monotonous when you continue to grow in self-awareness, self-contact, and presence with others. These qualities invite sexual energy and reject monotony. Mature people can have as many problems, sexual and otherwise, as others, they just manage differently by using problems as opportunities.

Suggestions:

1. Compare the next three pages by noting where you fit.

2. The information you glean from this exercise can distinguish your competent self from your overdependent self. If you observe closely, you may experience the discomfort in your potential for sexual growth.

3. Don't blow up, don't cave in, and don't give up. Just quiet yourself.

4. When you have finished the exercise, notice how thinking about disappointing sex, functional sex, and erotic sex affects you.

How Many of These Statements Describe You?

Dysfunctional Sex

☐ Chemistry is missing at all times, with all people.

☐ Arousal is incomplete or absent even with a strong emotional connection.

☐ Orgasms are absent, puny, or fantasy-dependent.

☐ Physical response to self-arousal is insufficient.

☐ Sexual desire for a partner is low or absent.

☐ You have disillusionment and disinterest in connecting emotionally.

☐ You blame others for sexual problems.

☐ You believe a better sex partner would produce better sex.

☐ You ignore or misinterpret signals for change.

☐ Sexual energy feels threatening to safety and security.

☐ You do not tolerate anxiety.

☐ You believe a partner should provide comfort, safety, and security.

Functional Sex

☐ Chemistry requires effort and is mediocre.

☐ Arousal is utilitarian, dutiful, or opportunistic.

☐ Orgasms are relaxing and occur at low levels of arousal.

☐ Physical response is present but passion is absent.

☐ Your desire is mostly utilitarian (relief, reassurance, etc.).

☐ You lose interest without knowing why.

☐ You notice no problem except monotony.

☐ You maintain your comfort level by avoiding risk.

☐ You don't like to gamble with the consequences of change.

☐ You restrict your sexual energy to one-night-stands, vacations, and unfamiliar but enthusiastic partners.

☐ You do not tolerate anxiety.

☐ When you have a partner, you each comfort the other against anxiety, or you leave.

Intimate, Erotic Sex

☐ Chemistry with the same person is present and changing.

☐ Arousal often has an erotic flavor.

☐ Orgasms are often powerful, connecting, and uninhibited.

☐ Your physical response is intact and often lusty.

☐ Your desire is to connect with yourself and your partner.

☐ You and your partner increasingly interest each other.

☐ You see problems as having meaning and potential to spur individual and relational growth.

☐ Discomfort signals growth and shifts the status quo.

☐ You tolerate and welcome change.

☐ You find increasing sexual energy as you develop in maturity and integrity.

☐ You tolerate, manage, and use anxiety productively.

☐ You soothe your own anxiety and tolerate that of others.

Notes

Closeness and Intimacy

Although people use these terms interchangeably, closeness and intimacy are different. Closeness allows you to know a partner better, and intimacy allows you to know *yourself* better, especially in relationship to another person. People thrive on closeness. Adults who are best friends before they become lovers often create lasting sexual relationships. Each cares about and knows the other so well that she or he can often predict the other's thoughts, feelings, and behaviors with fair accuracy. This establishes closeness, a familiar, comfortable, respectful, stable partnership. A flourishing sexual relationship contains large quantities of closeness.

Intimacy is different. The strange, soulful, uncomfortable, and unpredictable nature of intimacy makes it a lifelong, anxiety provoking, dependable aphrodisiac. Intimate moments are born from being aware of who you are, first, with yourself and, then, with someone else. *Intimacy requires you to be certain that you will not lose your sense of self in relationship to another person.*

A long-time familiar person who, at the moment, is strange, new, and unpredictable, is exciting. That is why the sexual experience of a new partner feels so stimulating, and why extra-relational affairs seem lustier than unchanging, stagnant, long-term relationships. In lengthy relationships, the depth of intimate moments can be so intense that people cushion them with affection and comfort (closeness). This can dampen ardor when emotional growth (unfamiliarity) lags behind familiarity.

Think about how you feel when you are the most intimate. Are you not deeply connected to yourself? Learning how to move back and forth between closeness and intimacy means moving back and forth between feeling safe and risking being known, wanting comfort and getting anxious, expecting the predictable and finding the unknown. Paradoxically, it is difficult to know and be known sexually and intimately. The lust you experience with a new partner is not intimacy, it is lust. Intimacy, like friendship, is developed over time. The experience includes allowing the best and the worst about you to be known by a person who could (but would not) shame you by knowing you.

These basic viewpoints can enrich your own experience of closeness (familiarity, comfort, predictability) and intimacy (strange, uncomfortable, unpredictable) and support an intimate, sexually active relationship.

Suggestions:

1. Read the next page to determine the differences between closeness and intimacy. If the ideas seem unusual, refer to the *Art of Intimacy* in Suggested Readings, page 109.

2. Think about how the notions fit or don't fit for you.

3. Don't blow up, don't cave in, and don't give up. Just quiet yourself.

4. Think about what it was like to consider new perspectives about closeness and intimacy.

Closeness in Relationship is . . .

☐ . . . familiar, comfortable, and predictable.

☐ . . . affirming and sustaining your partner.

☐ . . . partners validating each other.

☐ . . . when your partner is slightly more important to you than you are to yourself.

☐ . . . when your primary awareness is your partner's thoughts and feelings.

☐ . . . experiencing your partner in shared space.

☐ . . . intense interpersonal awareness of your relationship.

☐ . . . caring for and complementing each other.

☐ . . . gladly giving up portions of personal space and options so you can know the other more deeply.

☐ . . . necessarily negotiable because it involves behavior, and behavior is negotiable.

☐ . . . knowing your partner.

Intimacy in Relationship is . . .

☐ . . . unfamiliar, uncomfortable, unpredictable, unsure.

☐ . . . affirming and sustaining yourself.

☐ . . . self-validating, self-soothing, self-supportive.

☐ . . . being yourself without stopping your partner from being himself or herself.

☐ . . . relinquishing no part of yourself to bond with another.

☐ . . . experiencing yourself fully, in the presence of the other.

☐ . . . intense personal awareness of your relationship.

☐ . . . being willing to tolerate productive anxiety in the service of change and growth.

☐ . . . choosing to be truthful, compassionate, and related, simultaneously.

☐ . . . not negotiable because it involves experience and experience is not negotiable.

☐ . . . knowing yourself.

Purposeful Sexual Decisions

The key word in this exercise is "purposeful." The purpose, however, is not to get a prospective partner to be the person you are wishing for. The purpose is to accept yourself as growing and changing to meet your own desires. This exercise is to help you reflect on the kind of partner you want to be.

"But I can't be the kind of partner I want to be until I *have* one!"

The partner you always have, your primary relationship, is with yourself. As an adult, you can be the partner and individual you want to be. You can do this with compassion for your desires, rebellion against your values, or passivity toward your growth, but you do not need permission, approval, or even a partner, to be who you are.

This exercise offers thoughts about how you can be the partner you wish you were, or more of the partner in relationship you already are, to yourself and to someone else. You can enrich yourself sexually, and you can develop to the point where you like your sexual self.

The following exercise has five options. Select the option that best describes you:

"never," "rarely," "sometimes," "frequently," or "always."

You may dislike some of the items, but you will benefit from thinking about them all. Additionally, you will learn the most about yourself from items that stir you either positively or negatively. This means you are willing to observe your own behavior while you treat yourself with nonjudgmental compassion.

Suggestions:

1. Complete the exercise.

2. Observe how you handle discrepancies between how you behave and how you wish you could behave. Awareness of thought-feeling-behaving disharmony permits increased connection with yourself and ability to create harmony, if yours is low. Harmony happens when your thoughts, feelings, and behaviors are in tune with each other.

3. Don't explode, don't cave in, and don't give up. Just quiet yourself. Monitor your tension level.

4. When you have finished the exercise, think about what it was like for you to consider purposeful sexual decisions.

Purposeful Sexual Decisions

1. I actively listen to my intuition or inner voice about sex.

    never   rarely   sometimes   frequently   always

2. My sexual behavior feels self-respectful.

    never   rarely   sometimes   frequently   always

3. I express sexual frustration to a partner, gently.

    never   rarely   sometimes   frequently   always

4. I occasionally engage a partner with sexual enthusiasm.

    never   rarely   sometimes   frequently   always

5. I make time to be with myself, genitally, just me.

    never   rarely   sometimes   frequently   always

6. I am critical, withdrawn, or defensive about sex.

    never   rarely   sometimes   frequently   always

7. I stay present, talk straight, and handle whatever happens.

    never   rarely   sometimes   frequently   always

8. I stay with conflict until I get clear about the real issues.

    never   rarely   sometimes   frequently   always

9. I feel deeply connected to myself during and after sex.

    never   rarely   sometimes   frequently   always

10. I am emotionally responsive to my sexual energy.

      never   rarely   sometimes   frequently   always

11. Sometimes I use fantasy to distract or disengage.

      never   rarely   sometimes   frequently   always

12. I have enthusiasm for at least one exciting life project.

      never   rarely   sometimes   frequently   always

13. I live without sexual energy and wonder why it is gone.

      never   rarely   sometimes   frequently   always

14. Celibacy feels right to me.

      never   rarely   sometimes   frequently   always

Loneliness, Solitude, and Sex

Loneliness is basic to the human condition. To live fully we must eventually face this. The feel of existential loneliness can pull us into ourselves where, paradoxically, we can discover or disown how universally connected we actually are. Even though we all need the comfort of human contact, we also heal and renew in solitude. Accepting the joys of solitude sweetens human contact and softens living and loving, even in the face of sorrow, another aspect of the human condition.

Sorrow is one of the deepest of human connections. When, with courage and compassion (or kicking and screaming), we accept the reality of our aloneness, we can make deep contact with another person. Even in the depths of sorrow or frustration, contact offers temporary respite from loneliness. Suffering is created by self-defeating beliefs such as "Being alone is the worst that can happen," and dread of being alone, such as, "I will die, I cannot tolerate being alone." In western culture, we generate "loneliness anxiety" for ourselves. Unfortunately, we tend to equate loneliness with alienation and isolation, which are different experiences. You can certainly feel lonely without being alienated or isolated. However, the attempt to escape loneliness is far more alienating and isolating than facing it.

We have the paradox of two opposing relational tasks: learning to accept being alone and learning to accept being related. We must create opportunities to experience both sides of this paradox if we want to live as fully as possible. Solitude is a soulful experience by itself, beyond the task of confronting aloneness and connection. Solitude is the place where you go to heal and to enhance your spirit. Singles often have more solitude than they need, and couples often have less. "I feel especially lonely when I am sexually charged, in the company of couples, and have nobody with whom to express my love of life, even nongenitally."

Frustration and loneliness offer productive *and* immobilizing anxiety. Some genital urges are actually subconscious attempts to distract you from anxiety. Some are biological and cyclical. Some may be your body's yearning to revisit your unlived youth or your exciting or unexciting past. Quietly tolerating your sexual urges without acting on them can give you information about your unknown self. However, sitting quietly alone with the dread of being alone is not easily accomplished.

The frustration of a partnerless relationship is a fact of life from which you learn, lament, or enjoy, and learn some more. Missing a partner who left, died, or never existed in the first place can be an inherent sorrow that grieving does not always effectively relieve. Do not confuse sorrow with regret. Coming to terms with the sorrow in life is an act of hope, determination, and courage in the face of the inevitable end to all physical life. Yet, there is more to aloneness and solitude than frustration and healing. Although aloneness is something you manage, solitude is a sacred circumstance to celebrate.

Suggestions:

1. Complete the sentences in the next exercise.

2. Compare your responses to the idea of existential loneliness and loneliness anxiety. Which fits you?

3. Don't explode, don't cave in, and don't give up. Just quiet yourself.

Loneliness, Solitude, and Sex

1. I feel emotionally isolated when . . .

2. I handle that by . . .

3. Location is a major influence on my loneliness, as . . .

4. Social isolation, for me, is . . .

5. The hardest time of day/week/year for me is . . .

6. I handle that by . . .

7. I stay so busy that I don't feel lonely, and . . .

8. My sexual energy is the one thing I can depend on to . . .

9. The most important people in my life are . . .

10. Contact with important people is . . .

11. Major losses over the last five years include . . .

12. Major gains over the last five years include . . .

13. One cherished moment that outweighs my life's disappointments and betrayals is . . .

14. Even in loneliness, I can find something worthwhile to appreciate, for example . . .

15. Losing my dream of growing old with a partner is devastating/disappointing/motivating/irrelevant because . . .

16. Although I want a partner, I am not looking for one . . .

17. This suggests that . . .

18. I need to float on my loneliness for certain periods of time; it centers me by . . .

19. My solitude is so important to me that I rarely experience it as loneliness; yet when I do I . . .

Sexual Style

We do not usually consider sexual style as a royal road to the unconscious. Yet, sexual style is one way your subconscious mind communicates with you about how you live your life. Your style is based on old, learned values that repeatedly send signals about whether and how to be sexual. Although you may be aware of the way you enjoy sexual energy, express yourself, and find a partner, you may hesitate to explore what is not familiar, especially emotionally. Being able to tolerate the unfamiliar means you have to risk exploring the unknown. On the other hand, exploring the unknown means you are confident of emerging alive and unharmed from the experiment. While you can rest assured that your unconscious is always on survival alert, you may wonder how you create a sexual experience (or nonexperience).

Everyone has a sexual style (comparable to personality style) which may or may not mimic personality style. For example, an indecisive, passive person can be assertive sexually. A determined, dominating person can be shy sexually. More often, sexual styles follow personality patterns and reveal to you how you live your life in nonsexual ways. For example, a chronically angry person is not going to be a generous, sensitive lover. A gentle person is not going to become rough and demanding in bed. A timid, emotionally shy person will probably be the same with sexual behavior.

Your sexual style mirrors something about you, with and without a partner. With a partner, what you do the few hours before sex and during foreplay determines who, how, and what will happen next. A characteristic way of giving or receiving an early invitation for sex could include, for example, being playful, enthusiastic, hesitant, reserved, funny, aggressive, assertive, passive, teasing, seductive, romantic, expressive, self-confident, quiet, inviting, etc. Or, unfortunately, it might include being hostile, mean, sadistic, masochistic, tricky, pitiful,

73

fearful, guilt-ridden, pleasureless, self-serving, etc., or any other "wake-up call" behavior. Any one of these styles will produce results different from the results of other styles. And even though we don't like to hear it, we all have qualities that come across like the undesirable ones on the above list.

Expectations of pleasure and pain reveal your outlook about relationships and other circumstances in your life. The way you approach foreplay embodies your sexual style. For example, fear of punishment, rejection, neglect, and intrusion, can inhibit your reception of a sexual or other invitation. Expecting pleasure can enhance or disappoint, depending on whether you meet your expectations.

Foreplay has an unconscious component that communicates your behavioral intent. Examples of foreplay style include giving, receptive, skilled, smooth, lusty, tentative, conventional, imaginative, persistent, reliable, conscientious, dramatic, leisurely, sensitive, leading. Behaviors that force our growth when we meet them head on include indifference, selfishness, caution, inhibition, aversion, aloofness; these are the behaviors we think we can avoid in ourselves and others, right up until the time we meet them head on.

Foreplay and intercourse are as much physical expressions of what you want to say to a partner as they are demonstrations of technical skill. Intercourse style might include endearing, lusty, spontaneous, erotic, fun, serious, talkative, primitive, adventurous, irreverent, tender, loving, creative, insatiable, bonding, soulful. Less engaging behavior might include compliant, obligatory, dutiful, vigilant, intimidating, insistent, disconnecting, distancing, coercive, manipulative, or abusive. Sexual behavior can be as clear as words, and clearer. Your personal style with and without a partner is worth clarifying.

Masturbation is still a taboo topic in many circles. Yet, you uncover much when you examine your masturbation behaviors and fantasies with curiosity. The way you masturbate may contain a message about your personality and your sexual potential. For example: Do you make love to yourself, slowly, with intense arousal, teasing yourself to higher and higher sexual tension for as long as you want? Do you give yourself quick orgasms with low arousal simply for relief of tension? Do you stimulate yourself several times in a row without having an orgasm, and is this purposeful? frustrating?

Your fantasies are revealing, too. Fantasies can serve you well by connecting you with yourself, and poorly by detaching you. The question is, "How do my masturbation fantasies serve to connect me with myself?" The answer tells you whether yours connects you or blocks you from your own sexual self. Are your fantasies romantic, mechanical, masochistic, sadistic, coercive, dependent on the same ritual or theme? Is their purpose to manufacture an orgasm as fast as you can? Increase pleasure? Let you lose yourself? Fantasies can help you learn about your body and they can also help you tune yourself out. Fantasy-dependent orgasms during partner sex can tune out your partner. If you are having partner sex that is fantasy dependent, you might consider tuning in to your partner, as a variation.

We regularly find a partner whose sexual style pushes our own sexual growth. The consequences of childhood socialization, whether loving, neglectful, intrusive, or violent, often surfaces after the initial romantic-bliss stage of a relationship subsides.

Childhood fears (if you are aware of any) can be managed by purposefully engaging the internal "voice" of your competent adult self when you feel anxious, avoidant, and afraid. Claiming competence is an effective way to regain or gain control of the use of your adult body. Sex with yourself or another partner—if you look closely—will ultimately reflect your unconscious patterns and hidden personal growth opportunities.

Dealing consciously with anxiety enriches sexual energy. To have or not have anxiety is not a choice; anxiety accompanies both growth and stagnation regardless of your acceptance, rejection, or denial, of either. You choose the kind of anxiety you tolerate best even though you loathe or ignore the choice. Emotional security and growth does not require you to protect yourself or a partner from anxiety, give your self away, compromise your integrity, or embrace helplessness in order to connect with someone. When you face anxiety by self-soothing, self-validation, and self-respect, you choose mastery over dependency, consciousness over denial, and a chance for successful relationships both alone and partnered.

Sometimes your natural sexual self hides under layers and years of socialization. Reclaiming your right to your sexuality moves you into your adult, in-charge mode, often with anxious relief. As a competent adult, you manage your own anxiety. The gift in dissatisfaction is its motivation to acknowledge what you want and help you go after it.

Suggestions:

1. Create a list of words to describe your characteristic sexual style. If you are not aware of yours or have not had a sexual partner, list the qualities you have when you are sexual with yourself. If you do not masturbate or have no understanding of your sexual style, describe what this means to you.

2. Consider what your sexual style means and how it may have affected a previous relationship if you have had one.

3. Describe a sexual encounter you would like to have or change. The idea is to find desirable behaviors and attitudes, then consider how you might enhance yours.

4. Don't explode, don't cave in, don't give up. Just quiet yourself.

5. Think about what it was like to consider your own sexual style and pattern of relating sexually.

Characteristics of my solo sexual style:

Characteristics of my sexual style with a partner:

Patterns of Sexual Behavior

Apply the characteristics you just listed.

1. The first thing that happens is:

2. And then:

3. Here's how I predictably respond:

4. I do my predictable part anyway, because:

5. If I change the way I respond, then:

6. I would change this if:

Notes

Maturity

Because the term "maturity" has unique attributions and meanings to each person, you can make your own definition. Knowing what maturity means gives you behavioral options. Maturity does not mean boring, stodgy, austere, unsexy behavior. It means you are in charge of your life and responsible for the rewards and consequences of your own behavior when you are asleep, awake, playing, working, alone, and with someone, in other words, all the time. Here's how you might benefit from defining maturity for yourself:

1. Maturity is the quality that helps you avoid compliance, defiance, and indecision about sex and other issues.

2. Maturity helps you tolerate yearning for what you don't have, gives you courage to go for what you want, and equips you with the freedom and responsibility to accept, postpone, and decline other people's desires.

3. Maturity gives you the self-support to speak the truth and hear the truth, knowing it will push you to avoid exploding, withdrawing, caving in, and giving up.

4. Maturity gives you competence to inhibit the urge to defend, criticize, refute, or leave a promising interaction.

5. Maturity helps you avoid "no-growth" decisions and accept beneficial change even when it feels emotionally risky.

6. Maturity gives you resources for integrity and awareness, both of which are required before you can effectively invite sexual energy and a loving relationship into your life.

"Must I have a partner in order to develop maturity and integrity?"

No, but a partner will push your growth in almost every way you have unknowingly avoided since you became an adult.

On the other hand, only you can usher yourself toward your sexual potential. Nobody can manage your anxiety or make the choice for you between integrity and emotional comfort.

By now you should be familiar with one definition of maturity: "Don't explode, don't cave in, and don't give up; just quiet yourself." This means you contain but do not stifle your feelings as you listen actively, to others and to yourself. Containing your reaction lets you listen to yourself with intent and purpose. Being responsive instead of reactive means you can control your impulses instead of letting your impulses control you. Responsibility is the ability to respond, connect to yourself, be present, and accept consequences of your behavior.

Suggestions:

1. Make time to read the statements on the next page and add your own favorite characteristics.

2. Consider how you might enrich your own maturity and what this might mean to your self-respect.

3. Don't explode, don't cave in, and don't give up. Just quiet yourself.

Maturity includes the ability to:

☐ Soothe your own insecurity, anxiety, and fear.

☐ Maintain your own identity in the face of pressure to conform to someone else's idea of you.

☐ Manage your own intense emotions.

☐ Tolerate other peoples' intense emotions.

☐ Accept risk, ambivalence, paradox, and contradiction.

☐ Manage dissatisfaction and change.

☐ Stand as a separate individual at the same time that you bond deeply with another.

☐ Set your own limits with consideration for, rather than responsibility for, other people.

☐ Share the best and the worst of yourself with friends.

☐ Look inside and tolerate what you see, including faults.

☐ Be of good will in words and actions.

☐ Play often.

☐ Balance yourself when you are pulled off-center.

☐ Tolerate joy, grief, anger, fear, and orgasm.

Notes

Contradictions

Contradictions and paradoxes are normal, useful, everyday life events. A contradiction is an opposing, contrary, or conflicting opinion or event. A paradox is a statement or idea that is contrary to popular belief but that might actually be true. Both help people come to terms with emotional separateness, i.e., knowing you have your own thinking, feeling, and physical boundaries that nobody else can change for you; nobody else can know what being you is like.

Contradictions cause conflict and are useful for expanding your thinking. Managing contradiction is also necessary for personal growth. This does not mean stifling yourself or deferring to someone else "to keep the peace." Noticing and managing contradiction and paradox means you bring together seemingly conflicting ideas, beliefs, and goals. To see contradiction from a higher vantage point, you view one side of an argument as a possibility, the other side as equally plausible, and make them into another comprehensively different whole. Singles learn to observe internal conflicts by themselves, while couples learn to observe theirs together.

The statement, "I want somebody to desire me, but I would feel trapped by that desire," is a fertile contradiction that invites self-observation and conscious choice. Is "being desired" tolerable? Who imposes feeling "trapped?" Einstein said that you cannot solve the problem on the level of the problem. This means you rise above a problem to see the whole picture. For this example, feeling trapped is a function of what you tell yourself, not of another's desire, as it may seem.

"I want an intimate relationship where I control what happens." The contradiction is that intimacy and emotional control do not exist simultaneously. In lasting, healthy sexual relationships, emotional intimacy happens between peers, not between people who control or agree to be controlled.

85

Consciously accepting control of yourself removes you from a dependent stance. Being accountable to yourself shifts you into genuineness: "I want an intimate relationship where I am in control of me," is a statement of authenticity and possibility. In relationship language, this means you value your decisions and someone else's perspective. Creating "both and" instead of "either or" choices eliminates power struggles without erasing personal power.

Suggestions:

1. Read the next exercise and consider each item. Notice how easy or difficult it is to bring seemingly opposite sides of an issue together.

2. Don't explode, don't cave in, and don't give up. Just quiet yourself.

3. When you have finished the exercise, think about what it was like to consider contradictions.

Using Contradictions

I want . . .	And I also want . . .
A partner.	Solitude.
Self-reliance.	Dependability.
To love unconditionally.	To honor my requirements for loving.
To be loved and desired.	To be concerned about bigger issues.
To develop myself.	Growth in relationship.
Self-awareness and autonomy.	Suggestions and guidance.
To live in the moment.	To plan for the future.
Oneness with a partner.	To be separate and individual.
To work for self-awareness.	Rest from personal work.
Passion and intensity.	Friendship and reliability.
Erotic sexual arousal.	Companionship, peace, quiet.
To do all of this quickly; life is too short to waste even one moment.	There is enough time for this; life is to be savored slowly.

Notes

Thoughts about Sex, Celibacy, and Relationships

More than half of the single adults in the U.S. engage in sexual behavior, and more would if they had an STD-free partner. Others abstain voluntarily, even with a partner. Significant personal values and attitudes on sex, celibacy, and committed relationships has shifted since the advent of HIV.

Sexually active singles all the way from Generation Xers to sixties-plus are beginning to consider safe sex (not exchanging body fluids) as a variation of sensual and sexual pleasure. Single adults of all ages are coming up with clever ideas for sexual contact that doesn't include touching genitals. For example, using two condoms with lotion between the skin and each layer of latex is no longer a well-kept locker room secret! Men who are able to feel intense sexual pleasure using condoms are a masculine notch above those without the skill to sexualize energy so that erection is not overdependent on skin contact.

More people of both genders are now waiting until they have a lifetime partner for the experience of safe, penetrating sex. Positive results of preplanning sexual behavior instead of having impulsive, unplanned, unprotected sex are increasing, even though this may initially exclude "spontaneity." Falling down horny happens, certainly, but planning allows your values instead of your hormones to guide your behavior. It keeps you free from deadly as well as inconvenient sexually transmitted diseases. Preplanning sex (and no sex) increases self-respect, extends your chances for love and romantic involvement, physical pleasure, and orgasmic release. The last two do not require a partner. Negative results of sexual behavior are often the surprise outcome of impulsiveness and carelessness, e.g., unwanted pregnancy, sexually transmitted diseases, changed minds, disappointments and broken hearts.

Abstinence from sex, celibacy, is different from safe sexual arousal. Celibacy is the decision not to have any sexual stimulation at all, including self-stimulation. Many people use the term to mean no-partner sex, others include orgasm-producing self-stimulation with and without another person. Strict celibacy used to have very bad press except for the priesthood, with all sorts of erroneous beliefs about dire consequences, especially for men. The fact is that celibacy (with and without masturbation) is not harmful. Long unused, dormant genitals can be coaxed back to their former proficiency with masturbation techniques, even in very old people.

Some people who are strictly celibate do this as a religious calling. Others transform their sexual energy for use with creative projects as a way to honor individual values, break old patterns of thinking and feeling, and consider the joys of living without the interference of sex. Celibacy may help you find fascinating other aspects of life. Abstaining from partner sex while practicing masturbation may feel just right for some. Yes, not to be sexual is unnatural, but not *behaving* sexually is an acceptable human choice. Sexuality is about your being, not your doing.

Experience and age deepen your sense of those personal issues and life events that matter the most. The issue is not whether other people think sexual abstinence is right or wrong, but whether you are responsibly deciding how and if sex fits into your life at this particular time. Perspectives and values begin to shift as you grow in autonomy and experience.

Suggestions:

1. Read the next page. Discuss the notions with a friend or small group, if possible.

2. Don't explode, don't cave in, and don't give up. Just quiet yourself.

3. When you have finished, think what it was like for you to consider these particular ideas.

Thoughts about Sex, Celibacy, and Relationships

1. Unlike reproductive, casual, or briefly lusty sex, sustained, erotic sex is developed consciously, over time.

2. You deepen your ability to love each time you see yourself clearly and accept who you are aside from a partner's needs, wants, and beliefs.

3. When you love yourself, you invite intimacy instead of attachment hunger into your life.

4. In a loving relationship, you feel good about yourself most of the time.

5. Most people behave only as erotically as they believe a partner can tolerate. Others show off to impress you, without sensitivity.

6. Attention, compassion, conflict, and differentness can be effective aphrodisiacs in adult relationships.

7. Intense genital stimulation and orgasm are necessary but not sufficient for reaching your sexual potential.

8. Compliant and obligatory behavior lead to sexual apathy and resentment.

9. Sexual apathy is often an unspoken plea for presence when a person is here in body and absent in spirit.

10. No matter who has a complaint, nobody is innocent.

11. Until you can validate yourself, your dependency prohibits your erotic development.

12. You will utilize considerable self-observation, self-support, and self-soothing to become erotically mature.

13. "Monogamy" is a legal term that means having one spouse. "Sexually exclusive" means you are having sex with only one partner. Being sexually exclusive is a promise to yourself based on self-respect and fairness to your partner's right to know if you change your mind.

14. Loving and receiving love require acknowledgment and tolerance of impermanence and loss.

15. Generosity and good will are basic requirements for good relationships.

16. Each person ultimately decides whether to live life with fullness or with security. Accepting the inevitability of death allows you to have both.

With deep appreciation for personal communication over many years to anonymous research participants and: Drs. Carol Ellison, O. Spurgeon English, Joen Fagan, Richard E. Felder, Vivian Guze, Elaine L. Levin, Alexander Jasnow, Howard M. Halpern, Kitty LaPerriere, Thomas P. Malone, Natasha Mann, Frances Nagata, David M. Schnarch, Sol and Bernice Rosenberg, John and Elizabeth Warkentin, and Carl A. Whitaker.

Notes

Sexual Potential

Sexual potential is the highest level to which you can take your erotic energy. It includes your capacity to be deeply in touch with yourself mentally, emotionally, physically, and spiritually. This handbook is about stretching toward your sexual potential without a partner, with yourself as your primary relationship, a move that requires maturity.

Maturity is filled with paradox: It requires you to acknowledge yourself as you are now before you can move ahead. Maturity depends on your ability to soothe yourself, tolerate anxiety, manage pressure to conform, observe and use conflict and contradiction, and hold fast to your identity when feeling pressured by another person's needs. This is but the baseline leverage required to elevate your personal sexual potential.

Paradoxically, sexual potential requires you to acknowledge yourself as a whole being, not a defective who needs to change, while at the same time welcoming growth and change. You value and choose aliveness above emotional security, with and without a partner or prospective partner.

"OK, but, how does a person manage sexuality without a partner with whom to express it, without a relationship?"

Remember that your sexuality—your energy for life—reflects who you are, not what you do. By affirming your own mind, body, and spirit, you generate a passion for living. This passion for living is your sexual energy. Your willingness to connect with yourself mindfully, emotionally, physically, and soulfully is the actual challenge in reaching your sexual potential. When you claim responsibility for your own thoughts, feelings, and behaviors, you develop resources with which to change what no longer serves your growth and enrich whatever does. You then learn how to live with the resulting changes in yourself. This is not for the faint of heart.

Pushing your sexual self forward can feel risky, whether you are celibate or sexually active. You can feel more afraid of loss when you feel loving and juicy than when you feel dull and dead, especially in midlife and beyond. A "midlife crisis" reflects the discovery that you have a limited amount of time left to live. Little or no energy for yourself now maximizes the regret you may have when you get old. You can detach yourself from a full life in the present or you can risk feeling alive. Sexuality means feeling your aliveness. Genitality means feeling horny. If you feel horny, you can enjoy the feelings simply because they are your present experience.

By approaching sexual potential with maturity, you can discover what happens when you quiet yourself after you "Don't explode, don't cave in, and don't give up . . ." When you can acknowledge death as your permanent silent partner, you begin to live your life more fully than ever. Without seeking thrills, life becomes thrilling simply because you are alive and involved in life. Your internal "Wild Man" and "Dirty Goddess," archetypal masculine and feminine energies enjoyed by both genders, reinvent your sacred sexual energy, even, or perhaps especially, with voluntary abstinence.

Suggestions:

1. Read the next page. Notice which descriptions fit you. If you think, "I could feel more sexual if only . . ." note which behaviors you can claim as your own responsibility.

2. Don't explode, don't cave in, and don't give up. Just quiet yourself.

3. Think about what it was like to consider sexual potential.

Approaching Sexual Potential Includes:

☐ Being responsible to yourself, without pretense, including sexually.
(Integrity)

☐ The capacity to be caught off guard and enjoy the surprise and novelty.
(Playfulness)

☐ The ability to find fresh possibilities in familiar surroundings.
(Creativity)

☐ The occasional longing for the presence and absence of a partner, especially if you are in a relationship.
(Autonomy)

☐ The ability to play, be curious, be creative.
(Intimacy)

☐ Allowing your integrity to overcome and heal the wounds of childhood, alone and in a caring relationship.
(Maturity)

☐ The ability to observe and tolerate anxiety, ambivalence, and contradictions.
(Responsibility)

☐ Willingness to risk being yourself in new ways.
(Curiosity)

☐ Accepting the unchangeable rhythms and cycles of life.
(Surrender)

☐ Acknowledging impermanence and loss, yet living fully anyway.
(Acceptance)

Notes

Anticipating Loss

Nobody likes to do this exercise. It is number one on the most unfavorite list and the most revealing. Practice in courage is to choose sexual aliveness without, as well as with, a partner. Whether you are alone by choice or by circumstance, you may experience loneliness and disappointment, aloneness and solitude, and/or your life may be so full that you don't notice any negative results of being alone.

To remain single, be available but not looking, or search actively for a partner, are all choices, but we don't always get to choose. We take, gracefully or begrudgingly, what life hands us, but take it we must, we have no other choice. Regret, relief, sadness, denial, are but a few responses to the real losses of options as we pass midlife or encounter tragedy earlier in life.

Developing life and relationships as fate intrudes beyond our power to evade it can be bitterly disappointing. Misfortune and loss do not, however, wipe out your future opportunities to live a juicy life. The way you respond to losses of dreams, options, youth, trust, can renew your energy or drain you of it. You can choose the opportunities that energize you if you are willing to accept whatever life has to offer even though you don't like it, and risk disappointment in order to reach your heart's desire.

The passage through midlife and beyond carries the anticipation of loss. If you are in your early twenties and have lost a loved one, or lost part of your own development, e.g., your innocence before childhood was complete, you also know the grief of that passage. We lose many things in life: options, physical functions, friends, lovers, children, parents, homes, financial security, dreams for the distant future. Planning for the inevitability of loss helps you live more fully right now.

For example:

- If you desire, but do not have, a partner with whom to grow old, and if you grieve that loss consciously, you make space for new life energy.

- Youthful decisions and missed opportunities, as much as your successful choices, shape who you are today. Accepting those earlier choices, you can celebrate your present judgment. If you have ever erred and learned, you know that your errors and awareness of them gives you experience.

- Dreams die when you grow older with a partner for whom you have no sexual energy. Here, the choice is between despair and wholeness. Although you cannot go back to the past to create a different path, you can claim your own path now. It is never too late to repair or value your relationship with yourself. When you realize that you can be your full self in relationship, you can bounce yourself out of apathy by changing perspectives.

- When you elect to remain single, one door closes and another opens. There is always another door to open. Saying good-bye to a lover, to a way of life, to youth, to whatever you are leaving, is painful, but completing your good-byes allows room and energy for moving forward. Closing what is finished and opening new doors can bring the unexpected.

- Opportunity may be waiting for you to make a space for it.

- Realizing the power of your life force, look at how daring you are, or could be, right now. You can settle for your regrets or you can move forward with daring.

- Being mindful of life's inevitable endings can immobilize you. It can also urge you toward planning for your future and, thereby, your present. Rewards are bittersweet and the pain of loss can be deep. It's never too late to risk living gloriously.

Denying death deprives you of living fully. Practicing loss includes thinking about living your life without a specific or committed sexual partner. Your own death is a done deal. Your choice is how you want to live until then. Whether you plan for the eventuality or procrastinate, there are consequences. Whatever your age and however much time you think you have left, valuing life and planning for death is a developmental task.

If you are over fifty, think about the next decades and how you want to spend them. Think about growing old alone and what that means to you, how you will manage yourself emotionally and socially. With whom will you live?

If you are under fifty, think about what you want the next years to bring. Think about being alone and how you will manage emotionally and socially. Think about the possible feelings you might have, such as loneliness, peace, quiet.

Love is the partner of Death. The gift of life is going after what you want now, not despite the inevitable eventuality, but because of it. One could say love is foreplay for death. Loving yourself to life requires real aliveness—sexual energy—which is the true journey toward intimacy.

Suggestions:

1. Read the next page and then do the exercises.

2. Later, read what you have written. Reflect on the meaning of losing your dreams and changing your hopes.

3. Consider your plans for eventual losses.

4. Don't explode, don't cave in, and don't give up. Just quiet yourself.

5. When you have finished, think about what it was like to anticipate loss.

Anticipating Loss

1. Bring together some thoughts about your life and what the end of it means to you. Write your thoughts here.

2. Who will write your epitaph? What will they say about you? How do you want to be remembered? Do you want to be remembered?

3. Write a short note to your fantasied dead self. Include your appreciations, resentments, and regrets (in that order) about how you lived your life.

4. Consider whether you want to change anything about your life and how you might realistically plan that now:

Notes

Closing Comments

Sacred pleasure, the spiritual aspect of connecting with your sexual aliveness, is not addressed in this handbook. A growing process of loving yourself and your planet will lead you to discover the sacred meaning of your sexuality, your aliveness, and your aloneness.

Many, if not all, moments of self-connection feel sacred. Words to describe them are neither necessary nor relevant. Connecting to a higher power, and, through that higher power connecting with your sexuality, is a sacred act. Connecting sexually to yourself, and through that connection finding a higher power, is equally sacred. People report reaching this state through silent meditation, surviving great loss, love for people, work, music, art, nature.

Finding a way to unite your higher self with your life energy does happen physically. Tantra, as described in The Art of Sexual Ecstacy (see Suggested Readings, page 109), is an ancient Eastern science of spirituality expressed physically. Tantric sex encourages you toward sacred, blissful moments. It is worth exploring after you have developed the level of maturity and integrity required for intense erotic energy.

May the rest of your journey proceed with integrity, love, laughter, and knowledge of a life lived gloriously.

Notes

Appendix

Toning Your Orgasm Muscles

Toning the orgasm muscles enhances orgasms for men and women. Dr. Arnold Kegel in 1940 prescribed exercises to strengthen and tone the puboccoxygeal (PC) muscles of men and women who leaked urine (most often with laughing or coughing). The PC muscles are the ones that help you hold your urine, the ones that contract involuntarily with orgasm. Not only did patients report better urinary control, the surprise was that their orgasms got stronger or took place for the first time! Middle-aged, older people, and birth-mothers will find these exercises particularly useful. We now call these the "Kegel" or "PC muscle" exercises.

Men who exercise the PC muscles report more intense orgasms, increased ability to maintain erections, and increased ability both to delay and trigger ejaculation. Women report stronger orgasms and greater ability to trigger them. PC exercises can be practiced safely anywhere at almost any time except while driving or operating equipment that requires your full attention.

To identify your PC muscle: Imagine sitting on the toilet with your knees spread comfortably apart. Release and stop an imaginary flow of urine. The PC muscle is the only muscle able to stop urine flow in this position. When you recognize your PC muscles, you can exercise them in any position, unobserved: prone, sitting, standing, or walking. The only giveaway is the look on your face if you trigger an orgasm!

Like any other muscle, the PC gets painfully sore with too much exercise. Your goal is not to overexercise, but rather, to build muscle tone slowly, preferably over four to six weeks. If your PC muscles get sore, cut the exercises back by at least 75%. Check with your physician if soreness persists. The exercises can be done briefly, one to six times a day, divided into no more than five minutes at a time, and no more than fifteen minutes, total, in a day. Beginners should start with one minute or less and build to five minutes over several weeks. Remember to stop or rest when muscles tire. This exercise is designed to build pleasure, not endurance.

Exercise 1: Contract and relax your PC muscle rapidly, but not intensely. Begin with ten or fifteen brief, gentle contractions. Build to twenty-five the first week, fifty the second, seventy-five the third, until you can do about 150 at the end of a month or two. Then add Exercise 2.

Exercise 2: Contract the PC muscle, hold it in for four to eight seconds, then relax your lower body. Begin with five contractions and, gradually, over a few weeks, build to about fifty. When you can do fifty with ease, add Exercise 3.

Exercise 3: Imagine a ping pong ball rests at the opening of your vagina (anus, for males). Tighten your PC muscles as if to suck the ball slowly and deeply into the opening. Begin with about five strong "pulls" and slowly, in a few weeks, build to fifty.

Exercising the PC muscle is particularly important for women over 35 and for women who have given birth. Men lose PC muscle tone, too, with age. PC exercises help your orgasm muscles regain healthy tone. After you build tone by daily practice, develop a maintenance schedule of three times a week.

Suggested Readings and References

Anand, Margo. (1989). The Art of Sexual Ecstasy: The Path of Sacred Sexuality for Western Lovers. Los Angeles: Jeremy P. Tarcher, Inc.

Barbach, Lonnie. (1984). For Each Other: Sharing Sexual Intimacy. New York: New American Library.

Butler, Robert M., & Lewis, Myrna I. (1993). Love and Sex after 60. New York: Ballantine.

Dodson, Betty. (1987). Sex for One: The Joy of Selfloving. New York: Harmony Books.

Gordon, Sol. (1990). Why Love Is Not Enough. Holbrook, MA: Adams Media.

Gottman, John. (1995). Why Marriages Succeed or Fail. New York: Simon & Schuster.

Goulding, Mary M. (1996). A Time to Say Good-Bye: Moving Beyond Loss. Watsonville, CA: Papier-Mache.

Halpern, Howard. (1994). Finally Getting It Right. New York: Bantam.

Ladas, A., Whipple, B., & Perry, J. (1983). The G Spot. New York: Dell.

Malone, Thomas P., & Malone, Patrick T. (1987). The Art of Intimacy. New York: Prentiss Hall.

Malone, Patrick T., & Malone, Thomas P. (1992). The Windows of Experience. New York: Simon & Schuster.

Maltz, Wendy, & Boss, Suzie. (1997). In the Garden of Desire: The Intimate World of Women's Sexual Fantasies. New York: Broadway Books.

Morganthaler, John, & Joy, Dan. (1994). Better Sex Through Chemistry. Petaluma, CA: Smart Publications.

Ogden, Gina. (1994). Women Who Love Sex. New York: Pocket Books.

Schnarch, David. (1997). Passionate Marriage: Sex, Love, & Intimacy in Emotionally Committed Relationships. New York: W. W. Norton.

Shaw, Jeanne. (1997). Journey Toward Intimacy: A Handbook for Couples. Atlanta: Couples Enrichment Institute.

Shaw, Jeanne. (1998). Journey Toward Intimacy: A Handbook for Gay Couples. Atlanta: Couples Enrichment Institute.

Shaw, Jeanne, & Erhardt, Virginia. (1997). Journey Toward Intimacy: A Handbook for Lesbian Couples. Atlanta: Couples Enrichment Institute.

Stoppard, Miriam. (1992). Magic of Sex. New York: D. K. Publications.

Tieffer, Leonore. (1995). Sex Is Not A Natural Act & Other Essays. Boulder: Westview.

Zilbergeld, Bernie. (1992). The New Male Sexuality. New York: Bantam.

Community Resources

American Academy of Psychotherapists
P.O. Box 1611
New Bern, NC 28563
  Phone: 919-634-3066
  Fax: 919-634-3067
  E-mail: aapoffice@aol.com
  www.members.aol.com/aapoffice

American Association of Marriage and Family Therapists
1133 15th Street NW #300
Washington, DC 20005-2710
  Phone: 202-452-0109
  Fax: 202-223-2329
  www.aamft.org

American Association of Sex Educators, Counselors, and
  Therapists
P.O. Box 238
Mount Vernon, IA 52314
  Phone: 319-895-8407
  Fax: 319-895-6203

The Society for the Scientific Study of Sexuality
P.O. Box 208
Mount Vernon, IA 52314
  Phone: 319-895-8407
  Fax: 319-895-6203

Sexuality Information and Education Council of the U.S.
University of Pennsylvania, Graduate School of Education
3700 Walnut Street
Philadelphia, PA 19104-6216
  Web access: www.siecus.org

Your State Psychological Association
Your State Psychiatric Association
Your State Clinical Social Workers Association
Your State Nurses Association
Your State Licensed Professional Counselors Association

Your State Licensure Board (Psychology, Psychiatry, Social Work, Nursing, Counseling, Marriage & Family Therapy)

These resources can refer you to individual, couple, and sex therapists in your area, should you want consultation. Please be certain that any therapist you consider has credentials from your state licensure board. Credentials from national professional associations such as clinical membership in the American Association for Marriage and Family Therapy, and/or certification by the American Association of Sex Educators, Counselors, and Therapists will indicate expertise over and above a basic license to practice.

About the Author

Jeanne Slotin Shaw, R.N., M.N., Ph.D., is a grandmother, clinical psychologist, clinical nurse specialist, AASECT Certified Sex Therapist, psychotherapist in private practice since 1976, and Clinical Director of the Couples Enrichment Institute in Atlanta, Georgia. She has lectured and lead workshops for individuals, couples, therapists, and students in the U.S., Canada, Israel, and Australia, and is author of dozens of professional articles and four sexuality handbooks.

She is the creator of the Journey Toward Intimacy Retreat for Couples weekend and a regular presenter at the American Academy of Psychotherapists, American Association of Sex Educators, Counselors, and Therapists, the Society for the Scientific Study of Sex, the Society for Sex Therapy and Research, the Georgia Psychological Association, as well as various religious, university, training groups, and nonprofessional groups.

Notes

Don't Explode
Don't Cave In
Don't Give Up

Quiet Yourself

Couples Enrichment Institute
P. O. Box 420114, Atlanta, GA 30342-0114

Notes

Evaluation

Journey Toward Intimacy: A Handbook for Singles

Age_____   Gender_____

1. Please indicate your purpose in using this workbook (check all that apply):

   A. To help me explore personal questions or concerns.
   B. To find deeper relatedness.
   C. To satisfy my curiosity.
   D. Because a teacher/friend/spouse/therapist recommended it (circle all that apply).
   E. To update my knowledge for relationship, work, school, career (circle all that apply).
   F. Other:

2. Was the workbook personally beneficial?

   A. Not at all, a waste of time and money.
   B. Slightly, I got a little bit but not much.
   C. Moderately, I got something from it.
   D. Very much, I got a lot.
   E. Greatly, I had a transforming experience.

3. Did you complete all of the exercises?

   Yes   No

4. Which exercises were most valuable for you? How?

5. Which exercises were least valuable for you? How?

6. What would you like to have been different?

7. Are you interested in other sexuality workbooks?

    A. Couples
    B. Over 65
    C. Gay couples
    D. Lesbian couples
    E. Physical disabilities or medical problems

Other comments?

Thank you for taking the time to give us your feedback; your responses will contribute to ongoing research.

Please return this form to:

Couples Enrichment Institute
P.O. Box 420114
Atlanta, GA 30342-0114

Notes

Notes

Notes

Notes

ORDER FORM

Fax orders: (404) 255-7439

Online orders: forcouples@mindspring.com

Postal orders: Couples Enrichment Institute
P.O. Box 420114
Atlanta, GA 30342-0114, USA

Visit our website at http://www.mindspring.com/~forcouples/index.html

Qty	*Journey Toward Intimacy*	Unit	Total
	A Handbook for Couples	$12.99	
	A Handbook for Lesbian Couples	$12.99	
	A Handbook for Gay Couples	$12.99	
	A Handbook for Singles	$12.99	
$2.00 shipping for first book and $.50 per book thereafter			
Total			

Payment enclosed:

☐ Check (amount in U.S. dollars): $ _____

☐ _____   ____/____
    VISA or Mastercard Number   Expiration

Signature: _____

Print Name: _____

Shipping address: _____
                   Street   Apt. No.

_____
City   State   Zip

I understand I may return any unused, resalable books for a complete refund.

ORDER FORM

Fax orders: (404) 255-7439

Online orders: forcouples@mindspring.com

Postal orders: Couples Enrichment Institute
                  P.O. Box 420114
                  Atlanta, GA 30342-0114, USA

Visit our website at http://www.mindspring.com/~forcouples/index.html

Qty	*Journey Toward Intimacy*	Unit	Total
	A Handbook for Couples	$12.99	
	A Handbook for Lesbian Couples	$12.99	
	A Handbook for Gay Couples	$12.99	
	A Handbook for Singles	$12.99	
$2.00 shipping for first book and $.50 per book thereafter			
Total			

Payment enclosed:

☐ Check (amount in U.S. dollars): $ _____

☐ _____ ____/____
    VISA or Mastercard Number   Expiration

Signature: _____

Print Name: _____

Shipping address: _____
                Street   Apt. No.

_____
City   State   Zip

I understand I may return any unused, resalable books for a complete refund.

ORDER FORM

Fax orders: (404) 255-7439

Online orders: forcouples@mindspring.com

Postal orders: Couples Enrichment Institute
                  P.O. Box 420114
                  Atlanta, GA 30342-0114, USA

Visit our website at http://www.mindspring.com/~forcouples/index.html

Qty	*Journey Toward Intimacy*	Unit	Total
	A Handbook for Couples	$12.99	
	A Handbook for Lesbian Couples	$12.99	
	A Handbook for Gay Couples	$12.99	
	A Handbook for Singles	$12.99	
$2.00 shipping for first book and $.50 per book thereafter			
Total			

Payment enclosed:

☐ Check (amount in U.S. dollars): $_____

☐ _____   ___/___
    VISA or Mastercard Number   Expiration

Signature: _____

Print Name: _____

Shipping address: _____
             Street   Apt. No.

_____
City   State   Zip

I understand I may return any unused, resalable books for a complete refund.